re

rail

Text: Tony Bowerman

Series editor: Tony Bowerman

Photographs: John Street, Tony Bowerman, Carl Rogers, CWAC/Countryside Dept., Tom Bailey/Country Walking Magazine, Shutterstock, Dreamstime

Design: Carl Rogers

Ordnance Survey Licensed Mapping

Partner

Northern Eye Books

ISBN 978-1-908632-32-6

A CIP catalogue record for this book is available from the British Library.

Cover: Beeston Castle

Important Advice: The routes described in this book are undertaken at the reader's own risk. Walkers should take into account their level of fitness, wear suitable footwear and clothing, and carry food and drink. It is also advisable to take the relevant OS map with you in case you get lost and leave the area covered by our maps.

Acknowledgements: Warm thanks are due to John Street, onetime Sandstone Trail ranger, for his detailed knowledge of the area and its paths, and his kind suggestions of the best routes.

First published in 2016 by:

Northern Eye Books Limited
Northern Eye Books, Tattenhall, Cheshire CH3 9PX
Email: tony@northerneyebooks.com

*For sales enquiries, please call **01928 723 744***

 Twitter: @Northerneyeboo
@Top10walks

Contents

www.sandstonetrail.co.uk
www.northerneyebooks.co.uk
www.top10walks.co.uk

Cheshire's Sandstone Trail

CHESHIRE'S SANDSTONE TRAIL was one of the earliest middle-distance routes in Britain, and the first true 'Cheshire Way'. Carefully planned to take in the very best of mid-Cheshire, the Trail was officially opened in 1974. Not surprisingly, its popularity has grown ever since; and today, it's one of the most popular paths in north-west England.

In the early days the Sandstone Trail was far shorter than it is now, and stretched just 26 kilometres/16 miles between Delamere and Duckington, in central Cheshire. But the Trail was soon lengthened to cover 50 kilometres/32 miles between Beacon Hill, above Frodsham, in the north, to Grindley Brook locks, on the Cheshire/Shropshire border, in the south. The Trail was extended yet again in the late 1990s to link Frodsham, on the Mersey estuary, with the Georgian market town of Whitchurch, in north Shropshire.

Walkers admiring the view across the Dee valley to the Welsh mountains from Bickerton Hill

Along the wooded hills

It's no surprise that the Sandstone Trail and its well-kept side paths are hugely popular. In an essentially flat county, the steep wooded slopes, lofty viewpoints, dramatic panoramas, and sheer breezy drama of Cheshire's central sandstone ridge draw walkers like bees to honey.

Along the way, the Trail passes remarkable medieval and Victorian castles [see Walks 5 & 6], prehistoric hillforts [see Walks 1 & 3] and hidden caves [see Walk 9]. You'll discover half-timbered and sandstone farmhouses and manor houses [see Walks 7 & 8], old churches and chapels. You'll travel along a Roman road [see Walk 3] and medieval packhorse routes and saltways [see Walk 6]. Unmissable!

"The Sandstone Trail is an easy, well-signposted three-day family walk with a variety of terrain and wonderful views ..."

Hugh Baker, *son of Jack Baker, creator of the Sandstone Trail*

TOP 10 Walks: Sandstone Trail

HERE ARE THE TEN BEST SHORT, CIRCULAR WALKS along Cheshire's Sandstone Trail and the surrounding country. For the most part, the Trail hugs the high ground, making the most of every cliff path, cave, viewpoint and panorama. Yet nearby there is tempting, unknown country to explore. While these routes embrace all the traditional highlights of the Trail, they'll also give you unusual perspectives, and take you on unfamiliar paths to unexpected places.

Hillforts above the Mersey — page 8

Around Blakemere — page 14

Over the Old Pale — page 18

Kelsborrow Castle — page 24

Looking west to Wales from the top of Helsby Hill

Hillforts above the Mersey

Amazing views on a varied circuit around two prehistoric hillforts on Woodhouse Hill and outlying Helsby Hill

What to expect:

Several steep ascents and descents; woodland and field paths; Sandstone Trail; panoramic views

Distance/time: 4¾ miles/ 7.5 kilometres. Allow 2½ -3 hours

Start: Helsby Quarry car park, Alvanley Road (just off the main A56); halfway up Helsby Hill. Follow National Trust signs for 'Helsby Hill'

Grid ref: SJ 490 750 | **Postcode for SatNav:** WA6 9QE

Ordnance Survey Map: OS 1:25,000 Explorer 267 *Northwich & Delamere Forest*; OS 1:50,000 Landranger 117 *Chester & Wrexham*

After the walk: White Lion, Manley Road, Alvanley, WA6 9DD | www. whitelionalvanley.co.uk | 01928 722949 | broadoakpub@btconnect.com

Walk outline

From the old quarry car park above Helsby, the path rises through National Trust woodland to the breezy summit of Helsby Hill, with its prehistoric ramparts and panoramic views. The route then crosses the valley and follows the Sandstone Trail uphill through Snidley Wood to Woodhouses hillfort, high on Cheshire's wooded, central sandstone ridge. From the viewpoint at Scout Rock, the path drops down to recross the valley and climb the northern flanks of Helsby Hill. Back over the summit, the path heads down through the woods to the car park.

Helsby Hill 'trig' point

Helsby Hill

Helsby Hill and Woodhouse Hill have always been special. In prehistoric times their dominant summits — high above the Mersey Estuary — meant they were revered as sacred places. At first these cult sites may have been the scene of seasonal gatherings, celebrated perhaps with fires and feasts, ritual music, dance and sacrifice. Later, archaeologists suggest, they may have hosted specialised activities such as flint tool production, bronze casting and ironworking. Walk to their lofty tops today, and you can still feel the instinctive draw of these high places.

Celandines

The Walk

1. From the car park cross to **Hill Road South**, signed for 'Helsby Hill'. Enter the **National Trust woodland** at the top of the road. When the path forks 200 metres on, bear left, uphill, on the path to 'Helsby Hilltop'. It soon crosses the ramparts of **Helsby hillfort** to emerge on **Helsby Hill**, with its sheer cliffs and rock platforms jutting over the drop.

Head for the green-painted concrete Ordnance Survey 'trig' point on the summit. The panorama is astounding.

2. From the 'trig', turn sharp right, away from the edge, on a clear path that drops through the ancient ramparts to the National Trust boundary. Turn left at the T-junction, past **Harmer's Lake**.

Go through the gate alongside **Harmer's Lake Farm** and bear right on **Hill Road North**, which curves downhill past **Harmer's Wood**.

3. Two hundred metres on, turn right, through a footgate and onto a footpath signed for the 'Longster Trail' and 'North Cheshire Way'.

Turn left, through two kissing gates, bear left and skirt the edge of the field. In the far corner, turn left through another gate, and follow a **sunken way**, to emerge on **Tarvin Road**. Turn left, and head downhill on the road.

4. Within 200 metres, beyond **Teuthill House** but before **Bates Lane**, turn right, off the road, through a kissing gate signposted to 'Alvanley'. The path traces

0   0.5km   ½ mile

Mersey view: *The broad panorama from Scout Rock on Woodhouses Hill*

the field edge, crosses a ditch and heads left across the valley. At the bottom of the field, go through the gate and turn left, on **Burrows Lane**. Turn right at the T-junction, and walk uphill on the lane known as the **Ridgeway**.

5. Beyond **Foxhill Pumping Station**, bear left onto a bridleway signposted to 'Woodhouse Hill' and 'Frodsham'. For the next mile/1.5 kilometres or so, the route follows the waymarked '**Sandstone Trail**'.

Follow the sandy path, sunken in places, uphill through **Snidley Wood** to a junction at the top of the wood. Turn left here with the Sandstone Trail skirting the base of **Woodhouse Hill** — *topped by the eroded ramparts of Woodhouses Iron Age hillfort.*

The path bends to the left, around the northern end of Woodhouse Hill, before dropping down steps on the scarp slope to **Scout Rock** — a rocky viewpoint overlooking Frodsham Marshes.

6. Turn left, along the wooded lip of Woodhouse Hill. Just before a kissing

What a view: *Looking down over Frodsham Marshes and the Mersey from Helsby Hill*

gate into 'Woodhouse Hill Wood', turn sharp right, on a path that heads steeply down steps in a series of zig-zags.

At the foot of the hill, leave the woods and walk down the drive to **Tarvin Road**. Turn left and immediately right, down **Chestnut Lane**. At a **tiny ford**, cross the footbridge and kissing gate ahead. The path crosses a field and runs between gardens to **Profitts Lane**.

7. Follow the sign to 'Bates Lane' opposite. Cross the field and walk between gardens to **Bates Lane**. Turn

right and then left at the crossroads, uphill on **Old Chester Road**.

8. Less than 50 metres on, turn left again (before **Hillside Close**), up a narrow path signed to 'Helsby Hill ½'. The path rises beside gardens before climbing across the flanks of **Helsby Hill**. At the top, cross the waymarked stile ahead onto 'Helsby Hill' **National Trust land**.

Take the steeper left-hand path ahead, signposted for 'Hill Top'. Ignore the lower paths off to the right. The path curves uphill around the side of wooded Helsby Hill, then climbs more gently across the upper slopes of the northern scarp.

Roughly 500 metres later, the path crosses a spur of the **ancient ramparts** to enter the interior of the **Iron Age hillfort**. The path rises steeply away from the cliffs, with spectacular views back to the north and northwest.

Out on the open **summit** again, head for the **Ordnance Survey 'trig' point**. Walk ahead, along the edge of the hill. Cross the ramparts and walk back down through the woods to return to the car park and complete the walk. ◆

Helsby Hillfort

Fortified sometime between 800 and 500BC, this early Iron Age promontory fort was protected on two sides by cliffs that plunged 120 metres to the surrounding marshland. A double arc of earth-and-timber ramparts faced with drystone walling enclosed the hilltop to the south and east. A polished stone axe, leaf-shaped arrowhead, saddle quern, and early Roman sestertius coin have been found on the hillfort's northern slopes.

Tall Scots pines frame the path around the western edge of Blakemere

Around **Blakemere**

An easy circuit on forest tracks around huge, recently flooded Blakemere Lake, in the heart of Delamere Forest

What to expect:

Easy, flat lakeside circuit on surfaced forest tracks. Sheltered woodland paths, waterside seats

Distance/time: 2¼ miles/ 3.5 kilometres. Allow 1-1½ hours.

Start/finish: Linmere Moss Forestry Commission car park, off Station Road, Delamere Forest. Information Centre, toilets, bike hire, café

Grid ref: SJ 549 705 | **Postcode for SatNav:** CW8 2JD

Ordnance Survey Map: OS 1:25,000 Explorer 267 *Northwich & Delamere Forest*; OS 1:50,000 Landranger 117 *Chester & Wrexham*

After the walk: Delamere Café and Information Centre, next to the main car park. CW8 2JD | 01606 882726 | info@delamerecafe.com

Walk outline

From the main Delamere Forest Park car park at Linmere, the route crosses the Chester-Manchester railway line before cutting through the trees to the edge of Blakemere's huge inky lake in the heart of the forest. A simple circuit on flat, surfaced forestry tracks brings you back past the GoApe! tree top adventure to the visitor centre, café and car park.

Blakemere

Blakemere was probably open water in Saxon and Norman times. But when Delamere — the 'forest of the meres' — was gradually drained and planted with trees between 1793 and 1815, the old mere became first a boggy moss and then 'dry' land. However, the forest oaks and, later, Scots pines grew poorly; and in 1997, the Forestry Commission clear-cut 113 acres of the old peat moss. The low-lying ground 'naturally re-wet' and Blakemere returned to its ancient form — a vast, inky lake in the heart of the forest. Today, a popular footpath, bridleway and cycleway circles all the way around it.

Delamere Forest signs

Grey squirrel

The Walk

1. Leave the main **Linmere car park,** turn left on the narrow access road, and head back towards Station Road. Less than 200 metres later, turn left, and cross the **Manchester-Chester railway line** on a stone bridge. Walk ahead on the forestry road, past the metal barrier.

2. When the path forks, close to an uphill bend 300 metres farther on, turn right onto a narrower woodland path — signposted 'Linmere Trail – 2 miles'. Within 50 metres, bear right again at a minor junction and follow the path through the trees to the lake.

3. Turn left, onto a wide surfaced track close to the water's edge. This **perimeter path** makes a full, clockwise circuit of atmospheric **Blakemere**.

4. Three hundred metres later, continue ahead at a crossroads with a minor path, whose righthand arm vanishes into the lake close to a sign warning: '*! Danger – Deep Water*'.

Follow the lakeside track for the next ½ mile/800 metres to a four-way junction near the western-most corner of the mere. Bear right and continue on the broad track encircling the lake. *For a while Blakemere remains out of sight, hidden by dense forest.*

5. At the next junction, 300 metres later, look for a picnic table and bench beside the track. Opposite is a large two-armed signpost pointing to 'Whitemoor Gates' and 'Station Road', and right to 'Linmere Cycle Trails' and 'Delamere Way'. (The lefthand path leads to **Barns Bridge Gates** car park.) Continue around the lake on the broad perimeter track.

6. When the track crosses a broad drainage ditch at a junction with another narrower, uphill path on a bend, continue to the right, on the main, surfaced track around the lake. Up to the left is **Hunger Hill**. The path runs closer to the lakeshore along this northern side of the mere.

Black lake: *Ancient Blakemere was deliberately 'rewetted' in the 1990s*

7. When you reach another T-junction at the bottom, north-east corner of the lake, turn right, and walk on around the perimeter of the lake. For the next 400 metres the broad perimeter path winds through the trees between the lake and parallel **Station Road**. The main perimeter path bends gradually to the right, away from the road.

8. When the path forks at a junction, 300 metres later, bear left to retrace the outward route to the **'Go Ape!' ticket office**, **bike hire shop**, **visitor centre**, **café**, **toilets** and **Linmere car park**, to complete the walk. ♦

Dragonflies' delight

Blakemere's still, shallow water support twelve species of damselflies and dragonflies; and there are a further six at nearby Hatchmere, whose spring-fed waters are chemically quite different. That's a good proportion of the 23 species recorded recently in Cheshire. Key species at Blakemere include southern hawkers, ruddy darters and four-spotted chasers. Cheshire dragonflies are on the wing from mid-June to late summer.

The viewpoint and stone circle on Pale Heights, with Eddisbury hill on the horizon

Over the **Old Pale**

Around Delamere's hilltop medieval deer enclosure to the impressive ramparts of Eddisbury hillfort

What to expect:

Forest tracks and surfaced paths; field and woodland paths; Sandstone Trail; panoramic views

Distance/time: 3½ miles/ 6 kilometres. Allow 2½ -3 hours.

Start/finish: Yeld Car Park, Yeld Lane, off the A54 at the top of Kelsall Hill.

Grid ref: SJ 533 692 | **Postcode for SatNav:** CW6 0TB

Ordnance Survey Map: OS 1:25,000 Explorer 267 *Northwich & Delamere Forest*; OS 1:50,000 Landranger 117 *Chester & Wrexham*

After the walk: Lord Binning Gastropub, Chester Road, Kelsall CW6 0RZ | www.lordbinning.co.uk | 01829 751441 | info@lordbinning.com

Walk outline

From the car park on Yeld Lane, the path heads downhill to enter Nettleford Wood, on the edge of Delamere Forest. A surfaced path winds uphill to the modern stone circle and panorama atop Pale Heights. The route then crosses farmland to explore the ramparts of Eddisbury Hillfort, before returning along an old Roman Road back to Nettleford Wood, a section of the Sandstone Trail and the car park.

Eddisbury Hill

Standing guard over a prehistoric crossroads, Eddisbury Hill was strategically important in the distant past. Two long-established tracks met below the hill: a prehistoric ridgeway along the sandstone hills, and an equally ancient saltway through the Kelsall Gap. When the Romans arrived, they upgraded the old saltway into a military road — later called Watling Street — between the legionary fortress at Chester (*Deva*) and Manchester (*Mamucium*). Long after the Romans left Britain, the Saxons refortified the hillfort as a bulwark against marauding Danes.

Stand on the breezy ramparts today and you'll appreciate the ancient power of the place.

Path in Nettleford Wood

Meadow cranesbill

The Walk

1. Cross **Yeld Lane** from the car park. Walk down **Forest Gate Lane**, opposite, to a minor crossroads with **Morrey's Lane** and **Norton Lane**. Continue ahead for 300 metres to enter **Nettleford Wood**. Follow the track gently uphill through the trees until it meets the popular **Sandstone Trail** at the top of the slope.

2. Go straight ahead here, across the main Sandstone Trail, onto an alternative section of the Trail signposted to 'Pale Heights'. Follow the surfaced path uphill, through a gap in an old hedge, towards the trio of **communication masts** at the top of the hill.

Continue through another gap in a hedge, with the masts up to your right.

Fifty metres on, at a crossroads of paths, continue ahead on a rising path that curves past an old **civil defence bunker** set into the hill. At the top of the slope, bear left, and head for the stone edged platform at the northern end of **Pale Heights**. *It's topped by a clever series of standing stones representing the eight old counties visible from the summit. Several seats nearby are ideal for enjoying the panorama.*

3. From the summit, a path drops downhill to the right, beside a timber seat. *The trio of communication masts hugs the crown of the hill to your right.*

At the next junction of paths, continue straight ahead, downhill, on a path towards the forest. Go through the

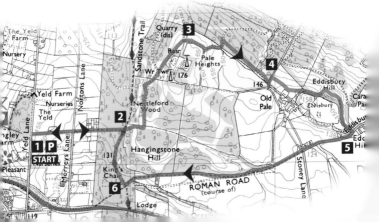

See forever: *Enjoying the panorama from the modern stone circle on Pale Heights*

gap in the hedge below, and turn immediately right, off the surfaced path, onto a broad track that runs along the inside of the hedge. Follow the slope gently downhill towards **Pale Heights Farm**, ahead.

Go through another hedge gap, ignoring a side path to the left. Instead, continue ahead for another 50 metres to a junction with a tarmaced lane. Turn left, downhill on this quiet, surfaced farm lane.

4. Within 100 metres, turn right, through a gateway, onto a grassy path. You're back on Open Access land again. Turn immediately right here, ignoring the lower path, and head uphill beside the hedge, towards the earthen ramparts at the northeast corner of **Eddisbury hillfort**, above. At the crest of the slope, go through the broad gap in the old hedge and follow the grassy path that skirts the contours of the slope.

The hillfort's massive double ramparts rise to the right, with grassy slopes falling away to the left.

Hillfort heaven: *The dramatic Iron Age and Saxon ramparts on Eddisbury Hill*

A hundred and fifty metres later, at the end of the ramparts, the path kinks sharply downhill to the left. Drop down to a broad grassy track.

Turn right and follow the path ahead as it skirts around the base of the hill. At the next junction, bear right and walk towards Eddisbury Hill Farm, ahead.

5. When the path emerges on **Eddisbury Hill Lane**, almost opposite **Eddisbury Hill Farm**, turn right. Continue past **Old Pale Cottages** and drop gently downhill.

When Eddisbury Hill Lane bends sharply to the left at the bottom of the slope to become **Stoney Lane**, continue through the gateway ahead, and follow the path along the field edge.

Go through the gateway at the bottom of the field, and continue along the edge of the next field. Soon, Old Pale Heights appears over the fence to the right, with the three communication masts crowning the hill above. Continue ahead, along the edge of **Organsdale Field**. *Look carefully and the line of the old Roman road between Chester (Deva) and Manchester (Mamucium) can be seen as a broad platform cut into the hill.*

Ignore the side path to the Old Pale to the right. Go over the stile into **Nettleford Wood**, and drop through the trees to rejoin the **Sandstone Trail** as it rises from the A54.

6. Turn right, on a broad path through the woods. At the top of the rise, 300 metres later, turn left at the signpost for 'Yeld Lane'. From here, the path retraces the outward route back to the **Yeld car park**, to complete the walk. ♦

Eddisbury Hill

Eddisbury hillfort occupies a steep-sided sandstone plateau. The earliest defences date from the late Bronze Age when a simple timber palisade enclosed the eastern end of the hill. The fort was subsequently enlarged to cover the whole hilltop. The fort was destroyed by the Romans, but reoccupied in the 4th to 6th centuries. The Saxons later refortified the site in AD 914 against the Danes. Today, most of the site lies on private land.

An unusual elevated path climbs to Kelsborrow Castle along the flanks of Boothsdale

Kelsborrow Castle

Up hidden Boothsdale to Kelsborrow's promontory fort, and round via a curious glacial meltwater channel in the forest

What to expect:

Gentle ascent and descent; footpaths, quiet lanes, woodland tracks and farmland; Sandstone Trail

Distance/time: 3 miles/ 5 kilometres. Allow 2-2½ hours

Start: Sandstone Trail car park, at Willington Corner, at the bottom of Chapel Lane, 1 mile southeast of Kelsall.

Grid ref: SJ 531 667 | Postcode for SatNav: CW6 0PH

Ordnance Survey Map: 1:25,000 Explorer 267 *Northwich & Delamere Forest*; 1:50,000 Landranger 117 *Chester & Wrexham*

After the walk: Boot Inn, Boothsdale, Willington CW6 0NH | www.thebootinnwillington.com | 01829 751375

Walk outline

From the car park at Willington Corner, the route heads up Chapel Lane and Gooseberry Lane to the foot of tree-fringed Boothsdale. At the top of this hidden combe, the path passes ancient Kelsborrow Castle, before rising along a lane to Primrosehill Wood. After a short detour to Urchin's Kitchen, the path returns past Summertrees Tearoom, Roughlow Farm and Willington Fruit Farm to Chapel Lane and the car park.

Boothsdale

Separated by 4,000 years, two very different groups of farmers have prospered on the sheltered west-facing slopes near Kelsall. Iron Age *Cornovii* tribespeople farmed narrow Celtic fields, or 'strip lynchets', on the steep slopes above Willington. Above them was Kelsborrow Castle, an earthwork and timber-palisaded hillfort overlooking Boothsdale. Modern fruit farmers were later attracted to the same slopes. Immediately below Kelsborrow Castle are the sheltered orchards of Willington Fruit Farm. Protected from icy east winds, and safely above the early and late frost line, the west-facing slopes of Cheshire's central sandstone hills are ideal for growing tender fruit and vegetables.

Boot to Boothsdale path

Foxgloves

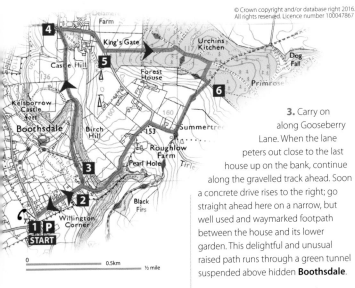

3. Carry on along Gooseberry Lane. When the lane peters out close to the last house up on the bank, continue along the gravelled track ahead. Soon a concrete drive rises to the right; go straight ahead here on a narrow, but well used and waymarked footpath between the house and its lower garden. This delightful and unusual raised path runs through a green tunnel suspended above hidden **Boothsdale**.

At the top of the slope, the path emerges into open pasture. Bear right, and head out across the fields, keeping parallel with the fence. *Across the field to the left here are the faint, eroded ramparts of* **Kelsborrow Castle**. *This late Bronze Age promontory fort takes advantage of the natural headland formed by Boothsdale on the southeast and the steep scarp across the fields to the west.*

Two more gates later, the path enters a narrow band of woodland, before opening onto a broad grassy area called '**The Waste**'.

The Walk

1. Turn right, out of the car park at **Willington Corner**, and walk uphill on **Chapel Lane**.

2. When the road bends sharply to the right, opposite the fruit farm, turn left into **Gooseberry Lane**.

Roughly 300 metres later, Gooseberry Lane kinks right and then left around the waymarked entrance to a narrow footpath that makes a short detour (roughly 400 metres each way) down to the nearby **Boot Inn**.

Ice Age oddity: Urchin's Kitchen is a glacial outwash channel hidden in the forest

Bear diagonally right across the grass, and cross the drive to join **Quarry Bank Lane** to the right of the bend.

4. Turn right, gently uphill along this quiet country lane. Past the pond, the road rises steadily then curves more steeply uphill to the right.

5. Over the crest of a rise, 50 metres later, turn left at a broad Forestry Commission parking area. A surfaced forestry track signposted for the

Sandstone Trail drops down the slope into **Primrosehill Wood**..

Ignore the path off to the left 100 metres on, signposted to '**Nettleford Wood**'; instead, continue downhill on the main forestry track.

At a junction of paths at the bottom of the slope, continue on the track as it bends around to the right. Within 50 metres, at the bottom of a slight dip, two minor paths run off to either side.

The main circular route turns right here, on a narrow footpath beneath the pines.

Distant horizons: *A broad panorama opens across the fields from the top of Sandy Lane*

It's signposted for the Sandstone Trail to 'Summertrees' and 'Beeston'.

(For a short but fascinating detour, take the lefthand path instead. A signpost points to '**Urchin's Kitchen**': *a narrow sandstone gorge scoured out by meltwater at the end of the last Ice Age.*

From Urchin's Kitchen, return to the main Sandstone Trail and go straight ahead, across the surfaced track, onto the narrow path beneath the trees. Less than 100 metres later, turn left alongside

the fence and continue uphill on the waymarked Sandstone Trail.

6. Close to the top of the slope, 200 metres on, turn right, up a short flight of steps and through a metal kissing gate beneath tall sycamores. The path follows the field edge uphill and continues through several kissing gates to emerge on **Tirley Lane** beside **Summertrees Farm**.

Turn right and, at the junction with **Waste Lane**, 250 metres later, bear left and follow **Roughlow Lane** as it meanders downhill past **Roughlow Farm**. Towards the bottom of the slope,

the lane curves to the right around cottages clinging to the slopes below **Willington Wood**. Within 200 metres, the lane rejoins **Chapel Lane** at its junction with **Gooseberry Lane**.

From here you can either return to the car park, and the end of the walk, at the bottom of Chapel Lane, or detour via Gooseberry Lane and its footpath to the **Boot Inn** at the foot of **Boothsdale**. ♦

'Boot Inn' or 'Cat'?

The Boot Inn was once run by Joe Lloyd, a real character who brewed good beer and told tall tales. Strangely, the old one-room Boot with its cosy fire was also called 'The Cat'. According to local legend, a policeman walked in on a poacher having a quiet pint. Quick as a flash, the poacher flung his dead rabbits into the flames. "Well, goodness me!", he said with a wink. "The cat's jumped in the fire!"

Victorian Peckforton Castle with medieval Beeston Castle behind

Cheshire's twin castles

A complete circuit of Beeston Crag — below Peckforton Castle — with changing views of the 'Castle of the Rock'

What to expect:

Sandstone Trail; flat farmland and fields; quiet lanes; canal towpath. Muddy in places

Distance/time: 3¾ miles/ 6 kilometres. Allow 2-3 hours.

Start: Beeston Castle car park (parking fee), Chapel Lane, opposite Beeston Castle gateway, Beeston, near Tarporley

Grid ref: SJ 541 591 | **Postcode for SatNav:** CW6 9UA

Ordnance Survey Map: OS 1:25,000, both Explorer 267 *Northwich & Delamere Forest*, and 257 *Crewe & Nantwich*; OS 1:50,000 Landranger 117 *Chester & Wrexham*

After the walk: Shady Oak, Bates Mill Lane, Tiverton, Tarporley CW6 9UE | www.theshadyoakpubcampsite.co.uk | 01829 730718

Walk outline

From Beeston Castle car park, the path follows the Sandstone Trail to Horsley Lane at the foot of the Peckforton Hills. It then heads over the fields, past Lower Rock Farm, to Bates Mill Lane and the Shady Oak pub. From there, it follows the Shropshire Union Canal to Wharton's Lock, rejoins the Sandstone Trail, crosses the Crewe-Chester railway line and heads back across the fields to Beeston Castle.

Beeston and Peckforton castles

Beeston and Peckforton Castles face one another from their respective hills. While Beeston Castle is a genuine medieval stronghold, Peckforton Castle is a clever Victorian fake. Designed by Anthony Salvin, an eminent Victorian architect who had already worked on the Tower of London and Windsor Castle, it was described at the time as "the very height of masquerading".

Beeston summit sunset

Ironically, when conservative MP and local landowner, Lord Tollemache, was building his replica Norman castle at Peckforton in the 1850s, he also lavished care on the real but ruined Beeston Castle. The simple reason? He wanted to improve the view from his brand new family home.

Peregrine pair

The Walk

1. From the car park, turn left along **Chapel Lane**. When the road bends to the left, go straight ahead on a footpath alongside the castle wall. The path drops downhill through open pinewoods.

The path soon opens onto **Tattenhall Lane** opposite **Tabernacle Cottage**. Cross the road to the left, and go up steps signposted to 'Burwardsley'. Follow the path across the field, cross the stream, and continue ahead along the edge of a second large field.

2. Around 200 metres later, turn right, through a waymarked kissing gate signposted for the 'Sandstone Trail'.

The path heads diagonally across the field towards houses tucked beneath the **Peckforton Hills** on **Horsley Lane**.

3. At the far side of the field, go through another kissing gate but don't turn left onto Horsley Lane. Instead, turn sharp right on a track beside the hedge of **Moat House Barn**. *New views of Beeston Castle open up ahead.*

Follow the track as it meanders downhill for 500 metres to a T-junction.

Go through the kissing gate directly opposite, and head across the field to another kissing gate in the far hedge. Then bear sharp left and head diagonally across the pasture to a waymarked kissing gate in the fence ahead. Join the farm track ahead, and continue alongside the hedge, now with Beeston Castle behind you and Peckforton Castle off to the left.

4. Around 250 metres later, just before a small wood, turn right on a signposted footpath and

0   0.5km

½ mile

Misty morning: *High on its crag, Beeston Castle is silhouetted against the rising sun*

immediately cross a wooden footbridge over a tributary of **Crimes Brook**. Walk ahead, with the hedge on your right. Continue past a field gate to a kissing gate at the top of the field. Follow the hedge ahead to emerge on **Tattenhall Lane** opposite **Lower Rock Farm**.

5. Turn right along the road and cross over immediately to enter the **yard of Lower Rock Farm**, between the farmhouse and its outbuildings. A wooden sign beside the entrance points

to 'Bates Mill Lane'. The public right of way crosses the yard to a stile in the fence beyond a tree-fringed **pond**. Please respect the privacy of the owners.

Cross the next field, passing another **marl pit pond** on the right.

Go over a grassy **estate track** and through the kissing gate ahead. At the far side of the next field, cross the boundary ditch on a plank bridge, then head for a waymarked post in the far hedge, to the right of the **brick cottages** ahead. At the waymarked post, turn right and follow the hedge

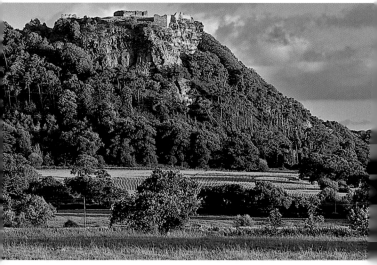

Seeing double: *Medieval Beeston and Victorian Peckforton castles face one another*

for 30 metres to a stile leading out onto **Bates Mill Lane**.

6. Turn left, and walk downhill past **Sidings Farm**. Over the railway, follow the lane past **Bates Mill** to the **Shropshire Union Canal**, and the **Shady Oak** pub.

7. But unless you fancy a drink, don't cross humpbacked **Bates Mill Bridge**; instead, go through the wooden footgate opposite the mill, and turn right along the **canal towpath**. Beyond the Shady Oak, opposite, the canal

follows the contours for 600 metres to **Wharton's Lock**.

8. Under **Wharton's Bridge**, head up the slope and turn right through a kissing gate signposted for the 'Sandstone Trail' and the 'Two Saints Way'. Cross the narrow **River Gowy** and head for the arch beneath the Crewe-to-Holyhead **railway line**. Continue to a waymarked post at the top of the rise, and cross the fields to a kissing gate beside a field gate. From here, the Sandstone Trail traces the field edge, before joining a cattle drive and heading for **Castlegate Farm**, to the left of **Beeston Crag**.

Below the farm, turn right, up steps and go through the kissing gate into the lane around the base of the crag. Turn left, uphill, towards Castlegate Farm. Continue past the farm and a narrow road on the left to return to the car park and complete the walk.

Don't miss a visit to the castle's lofty inner bailey with its panoramic views . It's a genuine Cheshire highlight. ♦

Beeston Crag

Beeston Crag has been revered since time out of mind. There's clear evidence of prolonged prehistoric settlement on the hill. One of its earliest names, Buistan, recorded in the Domesday Book, means 'market rock'. So, when the 6th Earl of Chester chose the crag for his castle in 1225, the site was already well-established. Beeston Castle adopted all the latest state-of-the-art techniques he'd witnessed in the Middle East during the Fifth Crusade.

Medieval Beeston Castle rises above a half-timbered Tudor house on Horsley Lane

Around the **Peckforton Hills**

Along ancient Horsley Lane, through the woods and over the wooded Peckforton Hills to ancient Peckforton Mere

What to expect:

Sandstone Trail; quiet lane; field and woodland paths. Steep ascent and descent. Muddy in places

Distance/time: 3 miles/ 5 kilometres. Allow 1½-2 hours

Start/finish: Large tarmacked parking area on the bend at the junction of Stone House Lane and Horsley Lane

Grid ref: SJ 538 582 | **Postcode for SatNav:** CW6 9TN

Ordnance Survey Map: OS 1:25,000 Explorer 257 *Crewe and Nantwich*; OS 1:50,000 Landranger 117 *Chester & Wrexham*

After the walk: Bickerton Poacher, Wrexham Road (A534), Bulkeley, SY14 8BE | www.bickertonpoacher.com | 01829 720226

Walk outline

From the parking area on Stone House Lane, head down narrow Horsley Lane — the old cart track around the eastern flank of the hill — before crossing fields to circle Pennsylvania Wood. The route snakes back up through open woodland, crossing the Sandstone Trail, to climb the 'Witches Staircase' to the crest of the Peckforton Ridge. It then drops past Peckforton Castle, hidden in the trees, to the gatehouse on Stone House Lane. From there, the path undulates across fields past Peckforton Mere to return through Willis' Wood.

Peckforton Estate

Once called the *'seedplotte of gentility'*, this part of Cheshire is home to a cluster of vast adjoining private estates, some dating back to Norman times. Largest of them all is Lord Tollemache's Peckforton Estate, which covers 28,650 acres (or 116 square kilometres). That's roughly *twice the size* of the Duke of Westminster's nearby Eaton Estate. Lord Tollemache built hundreds of estate cottages and promised every tenant "three acres and a cow". Overlooking it all is Peckforton Castle — an authentic, Grade I Listed copy of a medieval fortress high on Stanner Nab.

Peckforton Castle gateway

Tawny owlets

The Walk

1. Leave **Stone House Lane** and the parking area close to the bend, and walk down **Horsley Lane**. A sign says you're entering the 'Peckforton Estate'.

Soon the view opens out to the right towards **Beeston Castle**, high on its crag. Continue along the lane. For a while the route coincides with the **Sandstone Trail** — now signed for 'Burwardsley'. The lane passes **Moathouse Farm** and **The Moathouse**.

Continue past a smaller cottage. Ignore a track into the woods to the left, signposted for the 'Sandstone Trail'; instead continue ahead on the tarmaced lane. When it peters out

beyond **Woodend Cottage**, continue through the kissing gate onto a broad farm track that winds ahead beneath a line of gnarled and leaning oaks.

2. At the crest of a rise alongside the end of young woodland, turn right, off the track. A footpath sign points diagonally across the field towards the righthand corner of **Pennsylvania Wood**.

3. Enter the trees on a waymarked footpath that drops down to a boggy arm of open woodland. Cross a stream to emerge less than 100 metres later at another waymarked stile on the far side of the trees.

Castle view: *Flanked by oaks, Horsley Lane curves towards crag-top Beeston Castle*

Turn left and follow the waymarkers across the fields, keeping close to the woodland edge. Cross an old field boundary alongside the woods, and head for the far lefthand corner of the field.

4. Cross the stile and turn immediately left, uphill on a narrow path through pretty, broadleaved Pennsylvania Wood. Around 400 metres later, the path runs through a belt of conifers, to meet a (private) estate track.

5. Cross the track to a waymarked path opposite. The path traces the margins of the woodland ahead. At the top of the slope, go over a waymarked stile onto a track beside black-and-white **Pennsylvania Cottage**. Less than 100 metres on is a crossroads of paths where the route crosses the **Sandstone Trail** as it skirts the base of the **Peckforton Hills**.

6. Go straight ahead here, over the Trail, onto a narrow path that winds uphill beneath dark yews and hollies, then climbs giant steps sometimes called the 'Witches Staircase'. At the top, the steps

River cradle: *Ancient Peckforton Mere lies on the eastern side of the Peckforton hills*

meet a broad '4x4' track below **Stanner Nab**. Turn left here and, less than 50 metres later, right onto a waymarked path into the trees. The path drops downhill again through open woodland.

7. Beyond a **clump of yews** at the bottom of the slope, the path emerges on the main drive to **Peckforton Castle**. Turn right, downhill towards the **grand gatehouse**. Walk through the arch, cross over to the huge and ancient **Peckforton Oak**, and turn right, along the verge.

8. Less than 50 metres on, turn sharp left through a kissing gate hidden in the hedge. Bear left, andfollow teh well-used path around the edge of a large, undulating field towards distant Willis's Wood. (Ignore a side path off to the right towards **Peckforton Mere**.) Continue around the field boundary to enter **Willis's Wood**.

9. Follow the path through the woods ahead. At the far side, look for a waymarked stile. Don't climb over it; instead, turn left, and follow a narrow path just inside the woodland edge. The path passes two small ponds before emerging into the fields.

Walk along the fence, go over a waymarked stile, turn right, and continue towards a roadside gate in the hedge 200 metres ahead. Turn left along the roadside footpath and then, 250 metres later, cross the road back to the broad parking area at the junction of **Stone House Lane** and **Horsley Lane** to complete the walk. ♦

Peckforton Castle

Peckforton Castle is an authentic copy of a medieval castle built for Lord Tollemache between 1844 and 1851 for £60,000 (at least £8 million today). A Victorian contemporary described it as 'the very height of masquerading.' In an age of Chartist revolution, it was the last seriously fortified house built in England. Today, the Grade I Listed building is recognised by English Heritage as being 'one of the great buildings of its age'.

The charming hilltop Pheasant Inn at Higher Burwardsley

Pheasant Inn circular

A short but dramatic loop around the Peckforton Hills close to the Pheasant Inn at Higher Burwardsley

What to expect:

Quiet lanes, field paths, Sandstone Trail, woodland path, easy descent, woodland track

Distance/time: 1½ miles/ 2.5 kilometres. Allow 1hour

Start/finish: Sandstone Trail car park at the Cheshire Workshops, Sarra Lane, Higher Burwardsley

Grid ref: SJ 523 565 | **Postcode for SatNav:** CH3 9PD

Ordnance Survey Map: OS 1:25,000 Explorer 257 *Crewe and Nantwich*; OS 1:50,000 Landranger 117 *Chester & Wrexham*

After the walk: Pheasant Inn, Higher Burwardsley CH3 9PF | www. thepheasantinn.co.uk | 01829 770434 | info@thepheasantinn.co.uk

Walk outline

From the Sandstone Trail car park, the route passes the Pheasant Inn to trace the western foot of the Peckforton Hills on Pennsylvania Lane, before heading gently uphill on a woodland track. The walk then joins the Sandstone Trail, climbs obliquely up the steep scarp slope with views through the trees, before returning across fields to Rock Lane, above the pub. Quiet lanes curve back downhill to the car park and pub.

Higher Burwardsley

Higher Burwardsley grew up at the junction of two old tracks. One was the old cart road running around the western foot of the Peckforton Hills, represented today by Horsley Lane below Peckforton Castle and Pennsylvania Lane beside the Pheasant. The second route, which climbed over the hills via Hill Lane (also known locally as 'the Elephant Track'), was a lesser alternative to the main Salters' Lane or 'Walesmonsway' (now the A534 Nantwich to Wrexham road) that ran through the Bickerton Gap at Gallantry Bank.

Both these ancient saltways were used for centuries by long strings of packhorses carrying panniers of salt from the Cheshire 'wiches', or brine springs, at Northwich, Middlewich and Nantwich, over the Dee at Farndon and on into Wales.

Inside the Pheasant Inn

Cock pheasant

The Walk

1. Leave the **Sandstone Trail car park** at the **Cheshire Workshops**, turn left, and walk downhill on **Barracks Lane**.

When the lane meets **Fowler's Bench Lane**, less than 50 metres on, continue straight ahead down **Pennsylvania Lane**, past the **Pheasant Inn**. The lane winds downhill with wooded slopes up to the right. Ignore the waymarked side paths for the 'Eddisbury Way', which crosses the lane here.

Walk on past several houses set against the hillside. When Pennsylvania Lane ends at a metal gate, go through the adjacent wooden

kissing gate and follow the rough track gently uphill through the woods. Soon, the track rises between steep banks overhung by trees.

2. At the crest of the slope, turn sharp right, uphill on a lovely path that climbs obliquely up the steep, oak-clad slopes of the **Peckforton Hills**. Signposted to 'Bulkeley Hill', the path begins with sandstone steps beside a large boulder As the path rises, tantalizing glimpses of the westward panorama come and go between the trees.

At the top of the slope, the path emerges at a junction beside a bench. Ignore the path ahead, signposted to 'Hill Lane'. Instead, turn right, along the lip of the slope, on a gently descending path signposted for the **Sandstone Trail** — to 'Bulkeley Hill' and 'Rawhead'.

A hundred metres on, go through a wooden gate built into a drystone wall. From here the path traces the contours of the slope across two fields to emerge on curving **Rock Lane**.

Estate gate: *Entering Peckforton Woods on the Sandstone Trail above the Pheasant*

3. Although the Sandstone Trail continues straight ahead, we turn right, downhill on the gently sloping lane past a bungalow.

When **Rock Lane** merges with **Hill Lane** (known locally as the Elephant Track) at a fork, continue to the right, downhill, on the curving lane.

Around 150 metres later, at a minor crossroads with **Fowlers Bench Lane**, go straight ahead, on a short connecting lane, to return to the front part of the **Cheshire Workshops' car park** to complete the walk. ♦

The Pheasant Inn

The Pheasant Inn started life as a 16th-century working farm at the crossroads of two old tracks. Like many another wayside farm, they brewed and sold their own beer. James Wharton, the landlord in 1840, farmed 36 acres. The tradition continued until the 1950s, when the landlord of the 'Carden Arms' was still a part-time farmer. Renamed the 'Pheasant' in the 1970s, the Grade II listed pub still serves great food and real ales today.

A steep flight of steps climbs onto Willow Hill

Willow Hill & Sarra Lane

An unusual and varied circuit from Higher Burwardsley via the Pheasant Inn, Willow Hill and lovely Sarra Lane

What to expect:

Green lane, steep steps, woodland paths, quiet lanes, Sandstone Trail

Distance/time: 2½ miles/ 4 kilometres. Allow 1½-2 hours.

Start/finish: Sandstone Trail car park at the Cheshire Workshops, Sarra Lane, Higher Burwardsley.

Grid ref: SJ 523 565 | **Postcode for SatNav:** CH3 9PD

Ordnance Survey Map: OS 1:25,000 Explorer 257 *Crewe and Nantwich*; OS 1:50,000 Landranger 117 *Chester & Wrexham*

After the walk: Pheasant Inn, Higher Burwardsley CH3 9PF. www.thepheasantinn.co.uk | 01829 770434 | info@thepheasantinn.co.uk

Walk outline

Starting from the Sandstone Trail car park at the Cheshire Worshops, the walk runs past the Pheasant Inn before looping back across Higher Burwardsley Lane to Willow Hill. The path skirts through trees around the lip of the hilltop to emerge on leafy Sarra Lane, before crossing fields to Fowlers Bench Lane and the Peckforton Gap. The route returns along the hilltop Sandstone Trail to drop down quiet lanes to the car park.

Willow Hill

Willow Hill, near Higher Burwardsley, is one of the loveliest of the western outliers of Cheshire's central sandstone ridge. Like the main ridge, it's composed of Triassic sandstone laid down when dinosaurs roamed the earth.

There are veins of copper in the hills too, and by the Bronze Age, the people who lived here were burying their important dead beneath artificial mounds called round barrows, or 'lows'. Many of these 'lows' have since vanished; but their locations are recorded in local place-names all along the sandstone ridge. The name Wil-'low' Hill suggests it too once featured a Bronze Age burial mound somewhere on its top; but where, exactly, no-one knows.

Cheshire Workshops' car park

Barn owl

The Walk

1. Leave the dedicated **Sandstone Trail car park** at the **Cheshire Workshops**. Turn left, and walk downhill on **Barracks Lane**.

When the lane meets **Fowler's Bench Lane**, less than 50 metres on, continue straight ahead down **Pennsylvania Lane**, towards the **Pheasant Inn**. Continue down Pennsylvania Lane, past the pub.

2. Around 100 metres past the Pheasant Inn's 'Patrons' Car Park', turn left, down a narrow, ancient path that tunnels steeply downhill between the fields.

Soon the path opens onto a narrow, tarmaced lane called **Outlane**, leading to **Outlanes Farm**. Turn left, uphill for 200 metres until it meets wider **Higher Burwardsley Road**. Turn right, downhill, past a small sandstone cottage..

3. Roughly 100 metres later, just before the road forks at **School Lane**, turn left over a waymarked stile into **Willow Hill Woods**. Climb a long flight of timber-edged steps steeply uphill beneath the trees.

When the path levels off at the top, turn right beneath tall Scots pines and oaks, with sandstone rock faces up to the left. For the next 0.5 kilometres, this elevated path curves around the upper flanks of **Willow Hill** with constantly changing views through the trees.

The path dips and rises. Sometimes it's cut into the hillside; at others it drops down steps cut into the bedrock.

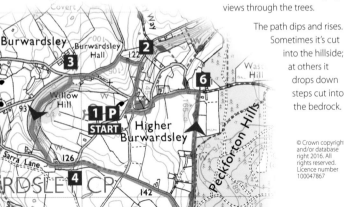

Lost lane?: *Pretty Sarra Lane curves up from Burwardsley around the back of Willow Hill*

When the broad path forks, go left, up a short flight of timber-edged steps onto the top of Willow Hill. Ignore the lower path, which continues around the contours of the slope.

Bear right at the top of the steps, beneath a gnarled oak. Over a stile, a new view opens out across the hilltop fields towards the Peckforton Gap and wooded Bulkeley Hill. Continue above a sandstone bluff, and drop downhill through a hawthorn thicket. Over a

further stile, the path drops beside a cottage. Cross **Crimes Brook** and go over the stile ahead, into **Sarra Lane**.

Turn left, uphill on the lane past **Quarry Cottage**. An oak topped sandstone bluff flanks the lane to the left; while down to the right is an old quarry.

4. When the lane bends to the left, less than 150 metres on, go straight ahead, over a stile, signposted to 'Fowlersbench Lane'. Out in the field, the path bends briefly to the left, curves around a boggy stream bottom, then heads out across the middle of the field. A waymarker

Natural high: *Willow Hill overlooks the church and outdoor centre at Burwardsley*

post, just beyond the crest of the slope, leads to a stile in the hedgerow ahead.

Go down steps into **Fowlers Bench Lane**. Continue ahead, on the righthand arm of Fowlers Bench Lane, up towards the **Peckforton Gap** and wooded **Bulkeley Hill**. The lane rises gently past occasional sandstone cottages.

5. At the top of the slope, immediately before the lane bends sharply to the right opposite **Peckforton Gap Lodge**, turn left, up stone steps, to a kissing gate signed for the 'Sandstone Trail'.

A broad path runs alongside a drystone wall at the side of the field. Continue through several small fields to a green tunnel beneath tall holly trees.

Beyond the enclosed path, a kissing gate open into fields. Follow the field boundary for 500 metres to go through a kissing gate onto **Hill Lane**. Turn left here, downhill on the lane, signposted to the 'Pheasant Inn' and 'Beeston'.

6. At the next junction, 50 metres later, turn right, on the 'Sandstone Trail'. Go past tiny sandstone 'Rock Cottage' and follow the lane as it curves around the beech tree-crowned hilltop to the left.

Ignore the next two paths off to the right and stay on the lane.

When **Rock Lane** merges with **Hill Lane** at a fork, continue to the right, downhill, on the curving lane. Roughly 150 metres later, the lane emerges at a minor crossroads with Fowlers Bench Lane. Go straight ahead here, on a short connecting lane, to return to the **Cheshire Workshops**' car park to complete the walk.♦

Cheshire sandstone

Cheshire's underlying sandstone was formed in Triassic times, between 225-175 million years ago, as layers of sediment washed down from the surrounding uplands by rivers and occasional flash floods. Iron in these sediments oxidised in the richly-oxygenated ancient air, creating the chemical 'cement' that binds the rock together. It's this iron oxide — or rust, as it's commonly known — that gives sandstone its characteristic colours.

Children perching on the isolated 'Droppingstone', near Rawhead

Rawhead circuit

Panoramic views from the highest part of the sandstone ridge with rock platforms, cliffs, caves and copper mines

What to expect:

Surfaced track, Sandstone Trail, elevated paths, quiet lane

Distance/time: 3 miles/ 5 kilometres. Allow 1½-2 hours.

Start/finish: Large roadside parking area at the top end of Coppermine Lane, off the A534 at Sandy Lane, Bulkeley.

Grid ref: SJ 521 551 | Postcode for SatNav: SY14 8BY

Ordnance Survey Map: OS 1:25,000 Explorer 257 *Crewe and Nantwich*; OS 1:50,000 Landranger 117 *Chester & Wrexham*

After the walk: Bickerton Poacher, A534 Wrexham Road, Bulkeley, SY14 8BE | www.bickertonpoacher.com | 01829 720226

Walk outline

From Coppermine Lane, the Sandstone Trail heads out past Rawhead Farm to contour the wooded slopes above Droppingstone Well and the Queen's Parlour. Beyond the Droppingstone's dramatic viewpoint, the clifftop path undulates along the lip of the scarp to the Trail's highest point at Rawhead. More cliff edge viewpoints follow, before the route returns past the coppermine chimney to Coppermine Lane.

Sandstone cliffs and caves

This breezy circuit of Rawhead takes in the loveliest, most dramatic scenery along the Sandstone Trail, with panoramic views across the Dee valley to the Mersey, the Welsh hills, Shropshire and the Wrekin. On a clear day you can see thirty or forty miles in most directions.

This part of Cheshire's sandstone hills has steep scarps, nose-like promontories, and occasional table rocks jutting over open space. The cliffs also contain several caves carved into the soft sandstone, with old folk names like Queen's Parlour, Bloody Bones Cave and Musket's Hole.

The 'Droppingstone'

Buzzard

The Walk

1. Leave the parking area and walk towards the top end of **Coppermine Lane**, where it meets the drive to Rawhead Farm. For the first half of this circular walk the route follows a section of the **Sandstone Trail**.

Head up the farm lane. When it bends sharply to the left beyond '**The Bungalow**', continue straight ahead, into the trees, on a narrower footpath signposted to 'Rawhead'.

2. Within 50 metres, turn left through a waymarked kissing-gate, and bear right on a path along the contours of the slope. Beyond a small **overgrown quarry**, the path rises gently across the tree-clad slopes.

Ignore a side path downhill to the right, and continue on the main path, waymarked for the Sandstone Trail.

Sandstone steps are followed by two longer flights before skirting beneath a prominent **rock overhang**.

3. Around 100 metres on, a short detour down wooden steps to the right leads to the unusual **Droppingstone Well**.

Return to the main path, and turn right. Soon, the path bends sharply to the left around the end of the escarpment.

Just before the bend, it's possible to scramble down the steep slope to an impressive, multi-chambered cave called the **Queen's Parlour**.

Man-made cave: *The Queen's Parlour was partly excavated for its soft scouring sand*

Around the bend, on the main path at the top of the slope, the ground falls away to the west, and the path climbs crude steps cut into the rock. Beyond a cottage-sized detached rock, known locally as the **'Moving Rock'**, the path rises to a breezy snout-shaped **table rock** jutting from the cliff top. Continue on the undulating path along the top of the wooded slopes. Ignore a lesser path, signposted to 'Harthill Village', that drops down sandstone steps through the trees to the right.

4. A few hundred metres on, the path rises to the white-painted, concrete Ordnance Survey triangulation point on the **summit of Rawhead** — the highest point on the Sandstone Trail.

Beyond the 'trig' point and a stone bench, the path veers left and right along the lip of the slope. Within 200 metres, turn right, to drop down a long flight of sandstone and timber steps above a **deep combe**. The path runs along the brink of sheer sandstone cliffs to a fenced promontory crowned by pines. The path bears left, past another sandstone outcrop and viewpoint.

Cheshire farmland: *Looking out over the broad Dee Valley from the 'Droppingstone'*

Ignore a waymarked side path to the right, and continue on the main path along the to another south-west facing sandstone viewpoint, this time with the Bickerton Hills clear in the middle distance.

Beyond **Musket's Hole**, the path undulates through open woods along the lip of the slope. Walk on past **Coomb Dale** and up to **Tower Wood**. Over the crest, the path hugs the field edge beside mature Scots pines, now with fine views east to the Pennines.

Follow the path downhill, and go through a kissing-gate beside **Chiflik Farm** to continue downhill on the farm drive.

5. When it bends to the right, 150 metres on, leave the drive and go straight ahead on a waymarked footpath along the field edge. A signpost points to 'Coppermine Lane'. Within thirty metres, turn left, and follow a signposted footpath above an agricultural yard. The path traces the contours, sidesteps through a wooded area, and runs downhill through a tunnel of trees on the edge of the fields.

Soon the path drops down a long flight

of steps to cross a stream. Climb the valley side and, at the top of the slope, turn right before the stile to explore the old **copper mine chimney**.

Return to the path and turn right, over the stile out onto **Coppermine Lane**.

6. Turn left and walk uphill on this quiet, leafy country road. When the lane levels out, continue straight ahead. At the far end of Coppermine Lane, roughly 500 metres later, is the parking area and the end of the walk. ♦

Copper in Cheshire

Copper has been extracted from east Cheshire's Alderley Edge since prehistoric times. Here, on the central sandstone ridge, copper ore was mined from the 17th century onwards. The first recorded shaft was cut in 1679; others were added in 1697 and 1735. Today, the tall sandstone chimney is all that remains of a pumping station built in 1856; the rest of the Victorian mine buildings were demolished by the Bolesworth Estate in 1928

Purple bell heather frames the southern view from Bickerton Hill

When the path emerges at an X-shaped junction of paths below the long flight of sandstone steps, bear right, slightly downhill and off the main Sandstone Trail, on a waymarked sandy path.

Turn right again at the next junction, and follow the main broad sandy track downhill to the main National Trust car park at the foot of Pool Dale, to complete the walk. ♦

Bilberries on the hills

Until the 1930s and '40s, when widespread hill-grazing ceased, Cheshire's sandstone ridge was mainly open heath with scattered trees. Heather, bilberry and gorse dominated the hillsides. When the bilberries ripened during the long hot days of July, local people and parties of Liverpool daytrippers flocked to the hills to picnic, play and pick the subtly flavoured fruit. Though most of the bilberries were eaten, some were sold at cottage gates.

Useful Information

Cheshire Tourism

Chester and Cheshire's official website covers everything from accommodation and attractions to shopping and family days out. See **www.visitchester.com/things-to-do.**

For Cheshire's best days out, see **www.favouritedaysout.com.**

Or visit **www.discovercheshire.co.uk** for detailed information on walking, cycling and other outdoor pursuits in Cheshire, including the Sandstone Trail.

Sandstone Trail websites

The comprehensive Sandstone Trail website covers everything about Cheshire's favourite long-distance trail, from walking directions to in-depth background information.

See **www.sandstonetrail.co.uk.** Or visit **www.facebook.com/SandstoneTrail.**

The Sandstone Ridge Trust is a charity set up to protect and enhance Cheshire's Sandstone Ridge. See: www.facebook.com/TheSandstoneRidgeTrust/

Sandstone Trail guides

You may also enjoy the *Official Guide to Walking Cheshire's Sandstone Trail* by Tony Bowerman, and *Circular Walks along the Sandstone Trail* by Carl Rogers.

See **www.northerneyebooks.co.uk** for details.

Tourist Information

Chester's Visitor Centre provides free information on everything from accommodation and travel to what's on and walking advice. Town Hall Square, Chester CH1 2HJ | **0845 647 7868**

Places to visit

Helsby Hill - Prehistoric promontory fort protected on two sides by sheer sandstone cliffs. National Trust. Scheduled Ancient Monument. Panoramic views.

Frodsham Hill - Prominent wooded sandstone hill overlooking the Mersey. Obelisk war memorial. Prehistoric Woodhouses hillfort. Panoramic views.

Delamere Forest - Cheshire's biggest woodland, popular for walking, cycling and horse riding. Visitor centre, cafés, bike hire and GoApe! tree-top adventure. **www.visitdelamere.co.uk**

Beeston Castle - 'Castle of the Rock', ruined medieval castle with panoramic views over eight counties. Visitor centre, shop, caves. **www.english-heritage.org.uk | 0800 015 0516**

Peckforton Castle - Authentic Victorian replica of a Norman castle, now a hotel, spa and restaurant. **01829 260930**

Bickerton Hill - Lovely, National Trust owned sandstone hills. SSSI. Restored lowland heath. Maiden Castle hillfort. **www.sandstonetrail.co.uk/walks-on-bickerton-hill/**

Weather

For a five day forecast for Cheshire and the Sandstone Trail, see

www.metoffice.gov.uk/public/weather/forecast/chester-cheshire-west-and-chester

Around **Bickerton Hill**

An elevated heathland circuit with stunning views — from Pool Dale to Kitty's Stone and Maiden Castle

What to expect:

Sandy heathland, woodland paths, gentle ascents, Sandstone Trail

Distance/time: 3 miles/ 5 kilometres. Allow 1½-2 hours.

Start/finish: National Trust car park (free), Pool Dale, Bickerton, up a sandy track opposite Pool Farm, Goldford Lane, Bickerton

Grid ref: SJ 503 531 | **Postcode for SatNav:** SY14 8LN

Ordnance Survey Map: OS 1:25,000 Explorer 257 *Crewe and Nantwich*; OS 1:50,000 Landranger 117 *Chester & Wrexham*

After the walk: The 'Sandstone', Nantwich Road, Broxton, Chester CH3 9JH | www.thesandstone.co.uk | 01829 78233 | info@thesandstone.co.uk

Walk outline

Starting on the eastern side of the Bickerton Hills, the walk rises across the heathery flanks of Pool Dale to the sandstone platforms near Kitty's Stone. It then undulates along the lip of the scarp to the earthen ramparts of the prehistoric ramparts of Maiden Castle with its broad panoramas of the Welsh hills. From here the route skirts the edge before looping back through open birch woodland to Pool Dale and the car park.

Rock platform

Bickerton Hill

Painstakingly restored by the National Trust, the Bickerton Hills are a deliberate patchwork of birch scrub, woodland pools and open heathland, ablaze in summer with purple heather, viridian bilberry bushes and yellow, coconut-scented gorse. This increasingly rare 'lowland heath' is an important habitat for rare butterflies and moths, beetles, grasshoppers, adders and common lizards. Combine this unusual natural richness with the ancient and atmospheric hillfort, some stunning panoramic views, sandstone outcrops, caves and promontories, and Bickerton Hill really is a special Cheshire place.

Common lizard

The Walk

1. From the National Trust's **Pool Dale car park**, ignore the main sandy track uphill. Instead, turn sharp right on a narrow waymarked path alongside a prominent information panel. Ascend sandstone steps up the valley side. At the top, go through the kissing gate and turn left along a waymarked track.

2. When the track reaches a signposted junction of paths beside an information panel on a sandstone block, 300 metres later, ignore the obvious path straight ahead, signposted to 'Rawhead' and 'Beeston'. Instead, bear right on a waymarked path that winds across the heath.

3. When it emerges on the main **Sandstone Trail**, turn left along the edge of the hill. *A breezy panorama opens out across the Dee Valley to the distant Welsh hills. Nearby is the curious memorial known locally as* '**Kitty's Stone**'. Follow the well-used Sandstone Trail as it curves left around the top of the slope.

4. Back at the 4-way wooden Sandstone Trail fingerpost, turn right towards 'Larkton Hill'. A sandy track drops between high banks. Go straight ahead at another wooden signpost that points across **Pool Dale** to 'Larkton Hill' and 'Whitchurch'.

5. When the path forks, bear right and climb the sandstone steps ahead. The path rises through the trees, and then climbs across open heathland to a log bench overlooking the Dee Valley.

0   0.5km

½ mile

August colours: *Gorse and heather on Bickerton Hill's restored lowland heath*

The path runs on, in a series of scalloped loops, to the ramparts of **Maiden Castle** prehistoric defended settlement. At the far side of the hillfort, drop down a short flight of steps to a major junction of paths.

6. At the foot of the southern ramparts, turn sharp right, downhill on a lesser, waymarked path surfaced with sandstone blocks. (Don't turn left along the track here, or take the broad path straight ahead.) When the path forks, close to the edge, bear left along the top of the slope. Ignore the steep path waymarked for the Sandstone Trail that plunges down steps to the right.

The lefthand path winds through the heather to another log bench with lovely views. Within 50 metres, continue through a kissing gate into **Hether Wood**. Turn right, on a well-used path along the top of the slope. Soon, the path drops diagonally down the hill alongside low sandstone cliffs. Keep to the main path to the bottom of the slope.

Hot, hot, hot: *Cheshire's oak-dotted farmland stretches away below Bickerton Hill*

7. When the path rejoins the Sandstone Trail at the foot of the slope, turn left, around the base of the hill. Ignore the kissing gate on the right, where the Sandstone Trail heads on south, and continue ahead on the path around the foot of the slope.

8. When the path forks 15 metres later, bear left, and walk uphill on a waymarked path to arrive at a low sandstone cottage on the brow of **Larkton Hill**. At the next junction, turn right on a waymarked access road.

9. Roughly 300 metres on, where the road bends sharply to the right, turn left beside the National Trust sign for 'Bickerton Hill'. Go through the nearby footgate and continue uphill on a broad track that rises towards the hillfort.

10. When the path bends to the left, 100 metres before the hillfort's earthen ramparts, turn right onto a narrower, National Trust waymarked path, which winds across the tree-dotted heath. Ignore a path off to the right, and continue on the broad path ahead. At the next junction of paths, less than 100 metres on, bear right on the broad waymarked path.